MALKIN

an ellegy in 14 spels by Camille Ralphs

illustrations by Emma Wright

'It is natural to unnatural people, and peculiar unto witchmongers, to pursue the poor, to accuse the simple, and to kill the innocent.'

– Reginald Scot, *The Discoverie of Witchcraft* (1584)

THE EMMA PRESS

First published in Great Britain in 2015
by the Emma Press Ltd

Reprinted in 2016 and 2017

Poems copyright © Camille Ralphs 2015
Illustrations copyright © Emma Wright 2015

ISBN 978-1-910139-30-1

A CIP catalogue record of this book
is available from the British Library.

theemmapress.com
hello@theemmapress.com

CONTENTS

PENDLE HILL

Now where is Demdike, old as toothache, she who
set two families to shelling stars like peas, who
firmly pelled the mell?

> *Helle*

And whose now is Elizabeth, her cross-eye set
high-low, unsoundable, – who onetime bricked a
cat into the wall, who frothed its bones to mortar
for the hours?

> *Ours*

And which of these is Alizon – the catalyst – who
cursed John Law but was blindsided when the
lameness flattened him, flung down a flyswat sky?

> *I*

And what remains of James – the son, the bumbler
scarved in pigswill – overleaping sickly faith to
come aground?

> *Grownd*

And what became the voice of Chattox, hers the tick-
ing, clapping teeth and lips, who lived by burgling
the Device dearth & wringing them of grain?

> *Rain*

And why the fall of Anne, the witch of images and
sculptor of the earth's slick flesh – who was at once
my Pendle's admiration and its terror?

Errorr

And what snapped loose when Alice – Catholic more than witch and highly-housed – was snatched from apse of splitting sun, refused to lapse to alibi & harm her friends?

Ends

And how well sing still Jane and John, took both for spelling mad one Jennet Deane; who, both on book as innocent, were dropped to dirt, to mouthfuls of black cob and furling cloudswell?

Well

And how might we hear Mould-heels, – stood accused of evil evil, housing thoughts as cold as empty beds – unscribbling the colic-common wind with baby's-cry?

Skry

And how in death lies Isabel, who followed up the scarp of sun and dubbed herself a witch (so the tongues of her wishes exalted and yodelled in air, then were stumped)?

Humpd

And where is Margaret, she who jinxed a horse as it collapsed, its legs a concertina; who lived, but to be dusted with bruises from dashed fruit and locked up for a year?

Here

And what the fate of Jennet, botch of Device batch
& birthed by Malkin Tower; – built on omens,
roof thatched with amens – who turned them in-
side-out, with all the rest?

>   *Arest*

These, in fog – subsumed – in earth as blood-filled
stones (chilling that unsweet syrup), dancing to
their own red music. Me, green as a symphony,
steepling off into tomorrow's air. You, fishing in
the dingle, in the rising of the waters, for a prize of
pillow-talk or humble pie, for the vast mirage of the
future – of voices hollow, small as flutes of grass.

Listen.

Elizabeth Sowtherns

(alias Demdike)

A boy gnew me by a stonepit. He steemed
in th sun stone-kneading, lighting trees like wicks;
his eyes were sofd as ash, and cities hymned
and chymneyed in the atlas of his sex.

I tricked in him, – unclocked all tocks, all ticks;
a debt that ploppd its anchor in my tchest –
nd 8 weeks fraille in rocking lihgt, I foamed
at the mouth like the sea. He ssuppd the moyst

unplundered of my underarm; he yessed,
impressed on me the braille of wouldlice
havocking the rocks.
                          I kept him at a cost:
he got with dogg my daughter, bent our howse
toward a future wigged with cirrus,
fingernail'd with hangman's lime. I died in prison.

ELIZABETH DEVICE

(daughter of Demdike)

Not fr a tick that very chyld
I dandlld on my knee, who never skorned
my one eyye bearing up, the other down –
my see-saw vizion, me
th pivot bungled in-betwene; who petted
'Ball' t herd the clowds, the gristle of the ages
in is teeth; who drankh
thikhly of evrything.

For when I gave my Jennet lynes
to summon drink, she marveled that
out back, the first rain clankd
sweet in th trof like a dog's barcking.

But when she spoke my spell
for them, the court, she brourt not ayle
knor mylk, knor wyne t frenzy on our roof,
but blood –
              Look!
see Malkin Tower molder in her skwall:
our home, my
other two loppsyded children,
mother bad-to-bone
riduced t kold and slopp,
nd a mongrel
yyammerringg.

6

Alizon Device

(daughter of Elizabeth Device)

Went beggin to begin wth, me; bt I was once
up Trawden Forest, blanketid in drisk, &
lifelike a trader passd me – jauntin his wrankle
of pack – & I askd: *You will spare
me sum pins, Mister Law??* Bt that man

kept his pace, & his pins! So, at my wish (a
fierwork f frown thrust up atop my head),
our cur – one a shrivll of detailes, th
pupil-soft tailes & th bluhot
abdominil blimpe – tailed him. It

slobberrd down, frazzzld th left
of his spine – w/ this hwiplash of tongge! –
w/ this fever tht chompd in th mustle! –
so his frame, cleft, sagged… He saw my anger's
blunt maw deepnning over him as he

spplinterdd in dirt… & I, at later siht
of him, untuckd these tears nd burnd to fix
his mallady. Bt I cud not; nd went out beggin
whyle th pluggin of my breth,
whyle I had nothing, nd nothing made sense.

7

JAMES DEVICE

(son of Elizabeth Device)

It was our Demdike rhoped me in to swindl
God out of a flaic of flesh… for her I ripennd in
the Maundy pew – I spunn the grubby penny of a
thaught inside my scul – imaginned wrenching off
His ear or Roman nose or the lovelorn tipp
of a finger – then staking it into the earth
in her devvl's bowwl… far too much to ask all this
of th boy without bread – wthout father – I –
I took the host and gulpd it down! nd led her imp
to hue n crye – to oathe to rupture me to fish
the limbs of Christ out semi-currdld frm
my popppopped gooseberry of belly… I crosst
myself – th creature petered out – but when
tht retch wreturned it naimed itself a bigger god
than mine I would dispatch into a bukkit
that same week – so oubt I shukkd the gubbins
of my soull nd – as a cretin – gave it up… at once
I felt the valleys shrunc to gutters cloggd
wth sky I saw a hare uneating embres
in th tumbledown of darck and rain spalling
the heavens as I stolle a littl lamb – and then
I saw the jury as they clappd me in the irons
of their eyes… I tolld them all of this – I swear
it was our Demdike rhoped me in to swindl…

ANNE WHITTLE

(alias Chattox)

Just *t csh* . - the once, my man – his skhul
sprorling with horns icy
as cenotaphs – gave up *csh t* - . to me a frumenty
with venison; a plush *csh t* - . manchet with
marmalade of quince; a djug of custard sloshd *t* ./ oevr
goose and peacock, lamb nd
potted beef – all set *t t* . ./ to work on unpikking my furious
wrinkls, or nhite-*t csh* . - swetting a slurry of plainsong above.

And after, well fed-up but famished, I knashed at th bare bakside
of an apl *csh csh* - -/ nd an appl &
another apple – and felt non the better for it, only old. Yet by
this bhlite *t t t* . . . nd my pan
of copper, egg white oracle, *csh csh csh* - - - I have second-
guessed *t csh t* . - . every future lottery: their
numbers rolllling over, sure,
continuus, and their hlopped *t csh t* . - . heads, sstopless *csh t csh csh* - . - -

ANNE REDFERNE

(daughter of Chattox)

In words, in images I came/I went
in klay of ashen hue. Man? Hare?
A long dewlap of rowpe? A hunt
inwards. In images, I came; I went
from such tuff dust nd fingerprint
to skyklad, krumbling, bluffd in air –
in werd, sin, images! I came, I went
in clay of ashh n human hair.

ALICE NUTTER

My home, in abbundance of breathy rooms –
so safe, the landings laffin th shutt
black box of a priest hole, sun blowin in

like a bedsheet –… then this: a cell, a crook
in rok, the place a tomb took root; a closure
that pothol d itself b twe n heads like

a louse, and my familly trikllng thik
frm my eyes, a confetty of ripppd
milk teeth. And weird deathbedfellows, all

of these: harelipppd by snott & trusssd
in naked sores, all sweating whites yolk-
yellow, shoose struk off like names… &

heere, my sleepe passsd in&out at odd times
in the day, like an amnesiak chambermaid.
My profecies, memories drownnd

in my follikles; nd when old Demdike lapssd
at last, we lifted her out like a stain. Only
later, – beyond the Assizes, as wynd nujd

my body's tchillld thurible – I swept off
to wait where the sun's Pentecostal nod looks
for you – each day – t bring bak my tongue.

JANE BULCOCK

Test I

You lok up our thumbs
with opposing tose nd then sling us, a hook,
t th watery snug – the rivvr, rust-
jungled with chainge, refuse, the curdld
recllect of stars; the rivvvr that lays
siege to us, only later to gush at our
throat like a mob n to swilll
      amung our dropsied
   glops of blud – to divine

              iff we'll giltily phloat. And we're damned
              if we do; and we,re certainly damned
              if we don,t.

       *

Test II

A grosse 5 iron inches –
longue, thik hairs pluckd
frm the cheek of an ore –
you sink in like a grief,

frakking for a numb spot
where the devvil plumbd
his tongue – for any lacuna
of sensitiviti, any bludless

sump. No birthmark,
no frekkl is left unvexd;
no eyelid left unflippd,
or body cavity unchekkd.

You had a right dogg's day
of the women you pitted
aggenst each other, pitted
liek oranj pomanders,

you bastards. Doornails!
Yr attempts to demarcate
th raized mole of Pendle
Hill have failed.

JOHN BULCOCK

(son of Jane Bulcock)

They are stil to shut up the open question:
all us who double-joynt justice. But be
u drawer or mothball-yn-drawerer of truth,
all lightnyngs dul & tuber yn th ground.

We swung by, th lesser of two eevls.
We yeelded a claptrappd washout – hyngeless,
fickle forecasts meted out like meteores.
We yeelded, a claptrappd washout; hyngeless
we swung, by th lesser of two eevls.

All lightnyngs dul & tuber yn th ground,
u drawer, or mothball-yn-drawerer, of truth –
all us who double-joynt justice. But be.
They are stil to shut up the open question.

KATHERINE HEWIT

(alias Mould-heels)

Her heavn-heavy daisychaine of bones…

Way back, I reasoned thence t me
nd mine, *What is a child discarded but a gapp-
tuthed calendar?* Yet my innocence (also)
stood out of the question – b yond it!

I murdrrd

tht girl as th cock churns th sunne
frm its grave; & thee ears on th con-
scriptid bodys – whisking ther bedsheets in
mirrorless rumes – cn only grasp dawn by tht call.

ISABEL ROBEY

As

        I

   listen:

               th wind

sinx a bhilllowing fist in th trees

the insects

are shrilll in my eers

           & away

fr m my cl thes nd my dr pt

       Os

of love I

breakneck

       harebrained

   flee –!

to th wood's
welter, safety of gnoise
& the bedlam of starrs
and my furr
ripppling like grey feelds of wheet.

But I shal be in a woman's likeness
                        evin now
            as ever I was,
        and everr shall be –

tho I shranc
as th ground

fell

beneeth me.

Margaret Pearson

So spoke, I felt, the note:

*

*Here flinches Margaret Pearson, welded, headlocked-up
in dribbling heft, this wreath of weathers, summoned
flung phlegm –*

> *A blak door in
> mye eye has brhistld open; not unsubtl,
> sumthing coming on… –*

*Deserving 4 distorting days, she'll wince in furnace-glare
of town, town, town; of our barricade knitted in skin; &
our hatred is one for this heifer passovered by cowpox –*

> *Unwinkd in sleape, I want not yr support so much as yr
> fier at my bak (ghet you behind me) –*

*And in the skirt-skew-whiffing winds, the improperly
groping winds His raspéd wounds abhorr'd, she
will be whip-licked, gilled through with the nick of time –*

> *& I implore you to hear the werd 'guillty' – to really
> heare it, as we and I hav done – just once, fr a tirede of
> years –*

*Witch-skipping o'er obsidian puddles, minced peat; the
latheralloʻer of heather: she has echoed unbridled her
stretchmarked ancient cradle, Ogden Clough –*

Fr I poulce in the smelting airr, the fields klinc in my rhist –

But now, the cleanslating rain

*

And my feet slerped the path. And my feet
slerped the path. Is all the world
a the, afoot. The feet hav slerped the path.

And my feet slerped the path. And my feet
slerped the path. Is all the world
derivativ. Sum feet hav slerped the path.

JENNET DEVICE

(daughter of Elizabeth Device)

A night at home: a borrowd
flesh was sslinking of the bone into
their mouths; & in congress a scrum
of tongss – contauting lode-
stonechat nd caterwaul – avowd
th gaoler should be killed, the bastard
castle doors be slautered on
their hinges... With such lines, I pickt

the sinful out, like stitches, from
th gossip-lacquered benches of the court:
I gushed at Alice Nutter, rang
the psalt-drop of her hand, nd Judast
all the rest. I had the choyce of life or
the devl and deth, which was
no choyce; and who but me can fathom
this long fosse of a fam ly grave, unreeling

(grasse trapdooring down) behind
at every step? I was r Demdike and
th ten blue-hangd of Pendle, then; I am
so still. They r so Legion, auditor;
so wintcrlesse, in flocks of
foxgloves hocketing the hill – tolling as
foreverly, as heavily n deadly,
as hell's bells. Please, forgive me.

NOTE ON FREE SPELLING

'Spell, my brethren, as you will! Awake, arise,
O language living in chains…'

– H.G. Wells, 'For Freedom of Spelling:
The Discovery of an Art'

———

Beyond the boundaries of orthodox spelling, a few effects can be achieved:

1. Semantic bridging: Polysemy – an opening of doors, within and between words; proliferation of meaning; a kind of lexical alchemy.

2. Visual onomatopoeia: A word or sentence may not only sound like what it represents, but look or behave like it, too.

3. Intensification by association: Colours/their associations affect our emotions in myriad ways (see e.g. Rothko's colour field paintings); likewise, certain combinations of letters are emotionally evocative.

4. Shock: Awareness of dissident spelling as an expression of identity, and of the immersive *umwelten* (or 'self-centred worlds') in the writing that results.

Each of these can be found within the poems.

ACKNOWLEDGEMENTS

Special thanks to Leo Mercer, without whom… etc. Also to Hannah Smith, Lenni Sanders and David Curley, for their invaluable early input, and to Emma Wright and Rachel Piercey, for their astute editorial suggestions.

Many thanks to BBC Radio 6 Music and Cerys Matthews for their kind invitation in April 2016, and to *The London Magazine, The Lancashire Telegraph* and Poetry By Heart, and to the reviewers who have taken the time to read and comment on my work since its first publication (thanks especially to *Sabotage Reviews* for their shortlisting of *Malkin* in the Saboteur Awards).

Thanks finally to me mam and dad, for generously supporting my suspect endeavours.

The source of most of my historical information is Thomas Potts' *The Wonderfull Discoverie of Witches in the Countie of Lancaster*. Further sources are Joyce Froome's *A History of the Pendle Witches and their Magic* and the 2014 BBC documentary *The Pendle Witch Child*.

The poetic form used here, that of the epitaphic monologue, is borrowed from Edgar Lee Masters' sequence *Spoon River Anthology*.

ABOUT THE POET

Camille Ralphs's debut pamphlet, *Malkin* (2015), was shortlisted for the Michael Marks Poetry Award and the Saboteur Award for Best Poetry Pamphlet, and featured on BBC Radio 6 Music, in a podcast from The British Library, and in various publications. She served as 2016-17 President of Oxford University Poetry Society, won the University of Oxford's Lord Alfred Douglas Memorial Prize, and edits the poetry section of the *Times Literary Supplement*.

ABOUT THE ILLUSTRATOR

Emma Dai'an Wright is a British-Chinese-Vietnamese publisher and illustrator based in Birmingham.

ENDNOTES

The following information has been drawn predominantly from the record of the court clerk at the time, Thomas Potts; the reliability of this as a source, however, is debatable.

Pendle Hill – Elevation 557m; located in the Pendle region of Lancashire, England.

Elizabeth Sowtherns (alias Demdike) – Demdike confessed that, while passing a quarry one day, she encountered a boy who demanded she give him her soul. Demdike said she used her relationship with 'Tibb' to lay down curses. She was one of the first witches to be taken to the castle, and died in prison before her trial.

Elizabeth Device – Elizabeth described her familiar, 'Ball', as a small brown dog; her daughter, Jennet, recited two of Elizabeth's spells to the court in a bid to prove her guilt. Thomas Potts writes that 'this odious witch was branded with a preposterous mark in nature… which was her left eye, standing lower than the other; the one looking down, the other looking up.'

Alizon Device – Alizon was a beggar by trade. The appearance of her familiar, a black dog with flaming eyes, allegedly brought lameness on a peddler Alizon cursed when he refused to help her. Upon seeing him in court, Alizon fell to her knees, confessed and 'with weeping tears… humbly asked forgiveness.'

James Device – James described how his grandmother, Demdike, sent him one Shear Thursday to get Communion and deliver it to a spirit on his way home. More than once, James refused the creature by asserting that his soul belonged to Jesus Christ; but the spirit, 'Dandy', told James that it was greater than Jesus Christ – and so James handed over his soul.

Anne Whittle (alias Chattox) – Following Demdike's example, Chattox said she allowed a spirit to suck upon her rib, after which a spotted bitch summoned a feast; when dining, the two never felt any fuller. Chattox accused Demdike of bewitching a number of people to death; Chattox was likewise accused by the Device household (the Devices thought they had been robbed once by the Whittles). Chattox had a speech impediment that caused her to stutter and make clicking noises.

Anne Redferne – Anne was acquitted at her first trial. When she was brought before the court a second time, her mother (Chattox) begged that the court show her mercy, but they did not. Potts writes of Anne that, 'had she lived, she would have been very dangerous: for in making pictures of clay, she was more cunning than any.'

Alice Nutter – 'A rich woman; had a great estate, and children of good hope.' She was also 'free from envy or malice'. Though the court records claim her presence at the Malkin Tower feast, this seems highly improbable: the Nutters were a Catholic family and she would likely have been elsewhere – perhaps at an illegal Catholic mass – on Good Friday.

Jane Bulcock – Jane and her son, John, were accused of cursing a woman to madness, based on a report from the Malkin Tower feast. They were anything but accepting of the verdict of their guilt (and are both recorded accidentally as 'not guilty' in the court record), and Potts describes them as 'crying out in very violent & outrageous manner, even to the gallows.'

John Bulcock – John was accused by Jennet of turning the spit at the Malkin Tower feast, though both he and his mother denied to the last their presence there.

Katherine Hewit (alias Mould-heels) – Reportedly, Mould-heels announced at the Malkin Tower feast that she had killed a small girl. She, like many of the accused, was picked out by Jennet as guilty.

Isabel Robey – Isabel allegedly told a number of local people that she was a witch and that she had bewitched or neglected to heal members of their families. Her reported words (including 'he shall never mend' and 'I have bewitched her') were wielded against her in court.

Margaret Pearson – The accusation in this case was the killing of a horse. Margaret's punishment was to stand upon the pillory in Clitheroe, Padiham, Whalley and Lancaster for one day each, with a paper on her head announcing her crimes; after this, she spent another year in prison, and then was allowed to go free.

Jennet Device – At the age of nine, Jennet acted as a witness against the accused, raising numerous accusations – including some condemning her own family. Although she walked away at first, her actions came back upon her: some years later, Jennet was accused of witchcraft by a ten year-old boy, and was herself placed in Lancaster Castle, possibly until the time of her death.

The Emma Press

small press, big dreams

The Emma Press is an independent publishing house based in the Jewellery Quarter, Birmingham, UK. It was founded in 2012 by Emma Dai'an Wright and specialises in poetry, short fiction and children's books.

The Emma Press has been shortlisted for the Michael Marks Award for Poetry Pamphlet Publishers in 2014, 2015, 2016, 2018 and 2020, winning in 2016. *Moon Juice*, a poetry collection by Kate Wakeling for children aged 8+, won the 2017 CLiPPA.

In 2020 The Emma Press received funding from Arts Council England's Elevate programme, developed to enhance the diversity of the arts and cultural sector by strengthening the resilience of diverse-led organisations.

The Emma Press is passionate about publishing literature which is welcoming and accessible.

Visit our website and find out more about our books here:

Website: theemmapress.com
Facebook @theemmapress
Twitter @theemmapress
Instagram @theemmapress

www.ingramcontent.com/pod-product-compliance
Lightning Source LLC
Chambersburg PA
CBHW071940020426
42331CB00010B/2955